Chiaroscuro

all my best!

Lori

Chiaroscuro

Lori Lucas

Copyright © by Lori Lucas

All rights reserved.
FIRST EDITION 2014.
FOURTH PRINTING 2019.

ISBN 978-0-615-98396-7

Designed and composited by Melissa Tandysh

All proceeds from the sale of this book will go to
Mental Health Partners of Boulder and Broomfield, Colorado

~ in honor of Rona ~

For David, Michael, Niara, and Zachary

CONTENTS

Chiaroscuro | 1

PART I ~ IN BRUSSELS

Brussels | 5
Moving Pictures | 6
American Woman Abroad | 8
Untitled | 9
Innocence | 10
Unborn Child | 11
Children of Hate | 12
Letters to my Friends | 13
At Jack's Place | 14
September | 15
The Mombasa Tree | 16
On Monday Morn | 17
A Child has Died | 18
London | 19
Rhodesia | 20
Progress | 21
Response to Yevgeny | 22
Niara | 23

PART II ~ AT ROSKO'S

The View from Rosko's | 27
Daydreams | 28
On Byzantine Rites | 29
Cambrian Way | 30
Punctuated Equilibrium | 31
Hallucogenia | 32
Late Last Night | 33
Now What? | 34
I Swear | 35
I'll be There | 36
Things, Only Things | 37
Patience 1 | 38
Patience 2 | 39
Luxembourg Ladies | 40
The Penitent | 41

PART III ~ BELLA CALMA TROVERA

Bella Calma Trovera | 45
Distance | 46
Please | 47
Little Wild Horse and Bell | 48
Nighttime in Goblin Valley | 49
The Tender Mother and the Melancholy Man | 50
The Circle | 51
Box Canyon | 52

CHIAROSCURO

The picture was begun a day too late.
Too many suns and moons around us set.
The lights and darks rose as a test to fate.
The colors I remember then forget.
What styles had we already set for those
We'd drawn into our lives before that day?
How many times must we pretend and pose
As if the darks and lights had faded gray?
Two figures hide beneath the shadows now
Obscured by charcoal dreams and memory.
As evening falls I often wonder how
This third dimension ever came to be.
The light against the dusk has now been drawn
And soon will come the dark against the dawn.

November 1970

PART I

IN BRUSSELS

BRUSSELS

An alien
Forlorn and lost
Swept across the sea
I stand searching
Unseeing and unseen.

November 1971

MOVING PICTURES

1. An old man approaches
   Passes the frozen roses
   His back forming a hard curve.
   He clutches the collar of his loden coat.
   He nears, passes the birdhouse
   Staring, head down, at the concrete squares.
   Stiffly passing on
   With tiny steps,
   Out of my sight.
   He is the poem, this old man.

2. Bald circle of a head
   With dark trimming round
   Left hand in pocket
   Hiding under blue grocer's coat.
   Right hand swinging down Rue Gratès.

3. Suivant—
   Soup truck, dressed dachshund,
   Deux chevaux, babushka, begonias.
   I wait for the slow parade to recommence
   While the leaves chase each other down the street.

4. Thin pink band around a gray curly head
   Quick steps with fists in pocket
   Of colorless coat.

5. Black plastic-buttoned coat covering housedress
   Scarf tied tightly under chin.
   Straw shopping basket in one hand
   While the other assures
   All buttons secured.

6. It's the man who lives behind us.
   Dominique's papa.
   He hurries home with the baby
   Wearing red over blue.

7. Two hands shoved deep down
   Into trenchcoat.
   A rhythmic motion of the body
   Carrying along head and hat.

8. Stub of cigarette perched in his mouth
   Hand clasped behind his back.
   He saunters, surveying the sidewalk.
   And glances at the old dog
   Crossing the street.

9. An open black wool coat
   Elbows flapping
   Hands flying in pockets
   Head turning from side to side
   Carried along by nerves and suspicion.

10. A self-confident walk
    Cigarette puffing, hands behind back
    Jacket unzipped.
    All seen before.
    Suddenly he turns and looks back
    Once
    Then again.

October 1971

AMERICAN WOMAN ABROAD

Jive-ass wagon wheeled mother
Cardigan-sweatered
Turtle-necked
Basic black-little b-mother.
Crib-married
Weekly-coiffed
Manicured Mom.
Card-carrying
Kent head.
Wedgie wearing, pant-suited
Panty-hosed Yankee Mom
With poodle-filled mind.
Refrigerated, beef-stroganoffed
Beaujolaised
French-fried mama
Jacqueline Susanned
Irving Wallaced
Tranquilized-aspirined mom.
Without Marx or Jesus or Che
Glass-cased, Key-ringed
Apron-stringed Mother
With streamlined fixed feline mind.

Spring 1972

UNTITLED

I take myself with me
Wherever I go
So I don't visit Pynchon or Berryman.
It seems that we're not both invited.

April 1972

INNOCENCE

My small son sleeps on
With his hand resting on my arm
His other hand half in his mouth
His eyes barely closed.
His clean dark hair looks newly combed
And lays straight across the forehead
I touch with my lips
I love this child —
The only testament to a possible god.

1972

UNBORN CHILD

Time was
When time stood still
And glided down
Before you came to share my life
And nights whirled in no direction.

Time is
When time dances
And glides forward
As you come to bring me life
And nights whirl gently all around.

Time will be
When it will bring
Another love for us to share
She will come when time comes
To bring her life.

May 1972

CHILDREN OF HATE

They watched and heard & learned
The prejudice & hate
And as children do
They yearned to imitate
They fought among themselves
In the name of god
They extended the horror
In response to a nod.
Some folks say it made them sick
(Like they did it on a whim)
The way they chased the soldier down
Surrounded & stoned him.
Their cheers were heard
Throughout the empire.
(They cheered as the soldier died)
How many parents
(Protestant or not)
Saw the truth that night
And cried.

August 1972

LETTERS TO MY FRIENDS

Dear Doug,
If I wrote you a poem for breakfast
Would you still want bacon and eggs?

Dear Rona,
Listen! You keep being different people.
If you could be only one for a while,
They'd let you stay.

Dear Mir,
When they called to say you'd died
I wanted to talk to someone.
And I nearly telephoned you.

April 1972

AT JACK'S PLACE

There is a feeling I get there—here
(From the red wine you'd say
And I'd agree, then object.)
There are some things to see here—
Like gold flying streamers
And red, white and blue bananas.
A tiny tv (off).
A rotating fan (on).
An orange Inno lamp
And boys in the band (who aren't).
Il est interdit d'interdire.

1973

SEPTEMBER

I'm sitting in a warm September sun
Listening to the birds applaud the day
Waiting for the sounds of morning's end.

I close my eyes and feel the sounds surround me.
The poem becomes a song and music moves around me.

1975

THE MOMBASA TREE

Harvest Morning
At the Sunrise
Eastern/Western Shores Dance
To the soulful forces of Al Rahman
Al Rahman

Fertile Morning
At the Dawn
Northern/Southern Stars Dance
To the Virgins' rites, Singing
God is All, God is All.

Namoli Morning
At Noon
Sun stands solemn
Saluting Sisters and Brothers.
Tribes of a Cosmic Black Universe
Sing Yen-Yere
Yen-Yere

Day Deflowers
Down the Dusk
To a Muslim Moon
To the Mombasa Tree
Native fruit of Namoli
And to Infinity.

1976

ON MONDAY MORN

Monday morning early in the year.
Snow on the January trees.
Everwhites embarrassed by the apple tree.
The sandbox now a skating rink for birds.
The cat is fat (pregnant says a friend).
The children built Chatbotté a house of bricks.
A crate for a roof, a blue rag for the floor.
A crèche perhaps to shelter the newborn
Away in a manger on Monday morn.
Is that the sun I see?
A Belgian sun?
I asked for one.

(1970's)

A CHILD HAS DIED

I heard a child died today.
Child of a mother born.
It seems he couldn't do his buttons.
And 3 weeks later he died
And 3 weeks later he died.

December 1974

LONDON

I saw a book of Victorian photographs today.
I saw a picture of London in 1874.
There was a traffic jam.

February 1975

RHODESIA

He put a rifle in his child's hand.
    Be careful now; it's dangerous.
    Don't go in front of a gun; it kills.
    You can have a try in a minute, dear.
For Christ's sake.

November 1976

PROGRESS

The number of blacks
In the Hall of Fame
Of Great Americans
Doubled today
To Two.
There is a long list
Of Losers
Like Sojourner Truth
Harriet Tubman
Frederick Douglass
Crispus Attacks
Benjamin Banniker
James Weldon Johnson . . .
But George Washington Carver
Was a winner.
Stolen from slave parents
And traded for a race horse.

1976

RESPONSE TO YEVGENY

No black blood runs in my veins
But I am as bitterly hated
By every racist as if I were Black
By this I am a human being.

NIARA

Tonight a strong wind delivered to me
The muted shrieks and desperate cries
Of Joshua lamenting
At a powerful pitch
As he went forth
To sound his strength
In oblong notes.

Then the wind died down and blew again
In stops and starts
To reveal in wonder
Joshua proclaiming . . .

Niara.

1972 and 1974

PART II
AT ROSKO'S

THE VIEW FROM ROSKO'S

Vehicles coming from every direction
Passing the trophy store waving its flags
Looks like the crossroads of Europe.
The café on the corner is full of men
Drinking Belgian beer at nine a.m.
Le Vicomte, Le Prevot, Chez Yanni
Just words in another language.
Not places you know or want to know.
The little square (a triangle really)
Entertains the birds and beloved dogs.
Old ladies carry marketing baskets.
They wear polyester dresses and lean on walking sticks.
A motorcycle buzzes by.
A gray Mercedes taxi makes a drop
At the photocopy shop across the street.
This a poem that could just keep on.
The only way to make it stop
Is to walk away from the window.

July 1990

DAYDREAMS

I dreamt I came to you
With my hair all pinned up.
I let it fall upon my shoulders,
And then it fell on yours.

Summer 1989

ON BYZANTIAN RITES

Leila would have liked to see
The four of us in company
Who made a pilgrimage to Rhode
To say farewell to her.
Catholic, Protestant, Muslim, Jew
Different native countries too,
Who came & went together
Stood & sat together
Watched & wept together.
Leila would have liked it.

November 1989

CAMBRIAN WAY

If our relationship was a sudden explosion,
It certainly had a very long fuse.

April 1991

PUNCTUATED EQUILIBRIUM

Scientists have a bias for gradual change.
They deal in 26 million year cycles.
So how could two months be considered long?
There is, however, this problem of the function
    of the incipient stages . . .

April 1991

HALLUCOGENIA

The path we follow has no rhyme or reason.
It is full of random change.
Its pattern unpredictable
Its evolution strange.
No slow or steady sequence
But a grand scale lottery,
An odd and quirky side branch
On the evolutionary tree.

Who will be the lucky winner?
The subset who survives?
Who'll be here when the sun explodes
Even the best design can die.

April 1991

LATE LAST NIGHT

Late last night by the dark of your room
I stood by the window in my winter coat
Looking out into the lamplit rainy street.
You lay behind me under a pile of wool blankets
Wishing I would go
Wishing I would stay
Wanting me to turn away
towards you.
Wanting me to see your green eyes
in the moonlight
filled with indifference
filled with desire.

November 1990

NOW WHAT?

The answer lies somewhere
Between all the words you've never said
And all the words I've written.

December 1990

I SWEAR

When you said Black Forest,
I thought, yes, I'd like to go.
We'll ride & drive,
We'll read & ride,
We'll see new things,
We'll laugh & joke,
Have a real good time.
Nothing else was in my mind.
I swear.
I thought we'd hike the trails
I thought we'd drink some wine
We'd stop & take a photograph
First one of me, then one of you.
It wasn't my intention,
I swear I didn't plan it,
It never even crossed my mind,
That after all the things we'd do,
That I would fall in love with you.

I'LL BE THERE

Think of me when you drink that last drop
of white wine in the kitchen.
Think of me when she touches you,
(or doesn't).
Think of me when you listen to BB King
or Sting or BRT
Think of me when you hike or bike or
ride in a boat.
Think of me when you go to Scotland or
The Ardennes or Australia.
Think of me when the clock cuckoos,
When the birds chirp like monkeys,
When you hear a goat's bell.
Think of me when you ride in a car
or on a jet.
Think of me when you stand by a river
or skip stones on a stream.
Think of me when you look at that big
farmhouse way far up on a hill.
I'll be there.

THINGS, ONLY THINGS

I see her face and feel her rising fear
Finding my gifts, my necklace,
The greeting card I wrote.
The Santa plate covered in cookie crumbs.

I watch her move from room to room
Finding my things everywhere
I wonder why she is afraid
For these are things, only things.

December 1990

PATIENCE 1

Leave him alone.
Let him be.
He may himself
Come looking for me.
And if he does not
He's not the one.
Leave him alone.
He may still come.

1991

PATIENCE 2

I'm not cutting my hair.
I'm not wearing fragrance.
I'm waiting for you to choose.

1991

LUXEMBOURG LADIES

Luxembourg ladies wearing hats
    & waiting for buses.
Silly signs saying Bofferding
    & Bofferdang.
Long red bridges on stilts
    extending over ravines
Banks & bridges & beige
    buildings all looking alike.
Listening to Handel's Messiah
    while stroking your silly hair
Laughing at your bad jokes
You're $4/4$ ths of a ghost
    (not a goat!)
Taking your picture in bed.

THE PENITENT

I went barefoot to the fountain.
I stumbled at the wall.
I could feel myself falling,
So I let myself fall.
You lifted me like Jesus,
Like Jesus from the cross.
And covered me with sacking,
Feeling sorrow for your loss.

~ PART III
BELLA CALMA TROVERA

BELLA CALMA TROVERA

I

Like a game
They start out light and gay
Then become serious, interior.
They find what they had waited for
All their lives.

II

All hope is gone.
They take out their guts and stare at them.
They make a downward spiral into chaos.
They see the tyranny of deceptions
By which they live.

III

At the end
They scream that they will find
The beautiful calm they have all lost.

April 1991

DISTANCE

I think you touched me
Once
Last Saturday night, it was.
When you adjusted
The tag on my t-shirt
Then again,
You did lay your hand on my back
For a moment
Down in the kitchen this morning.

August 1993

PLEASE

It's really not so bad
Living apart like this
With you downstairs & me up
We meet in the middle for meals
And make polite conversation.

August 1993

LITTLE WILD HORSE AND BELL

We made our way through the Narrows.
Climbing the cliffs and crawling on the canyon walls,
Carrying our packs through dry creek beds,
Complimenting the cottonwoods and the cacti,
Cursing the tamarisk and the deer flies.

May 1993

NIGHTTIME IN GOBLIN VALLEY

The half-moon and her sister
Shone down on us
From a clear Utah sky.
The gully side gazed
As we sat around
The circle of rocks.
The cottonwoods sang us their night song.

May 1993

THE TENDER MOTHER
AND THE MELANCHOLY MAN

I shall surround you with peace
So that you will neither fear
What you long for
Nor long for what you fear.

1993

THE CIRCLE

As I descend the stairs
and turn into the kitchen,
I catch sight of your leg,
as you leave the kitchen
to turn into the living room
to ascend the stairs.

BOX CANYON

You lured me and pursued me
Until I fell in love
But you would not love me
So I tried to leave
But by that time
There was no escape.

May 1993

ABOUT THE AUTHOR

Lori lives in Boulder, Colorado with Bob, Princess, and Pussy Kitty Big Boy.

Author Photograph: © Niara